SLUSHPILE MEMORIES

SLUSHPILE MEMORIES

HOW NOT TO GET REJECTED

KEVIN J. ANDERSON

WFP
WORDFIRE PRESS

EBook ISBN: 978-1-68057-297-1
Trade Paperback ISBN: 978-1-68057-296-4
Cover design by Janet McDonald
Cover artwork images by Adobe Stock
Published by WordFire Press, LLC
PO Box 1840
Monument CO 80132
Kevin J. Anderson & Rebecca Moesta, Publishers
WordFire Press eBook Edition 2022
WordFire Press Trade Paperback Edition 2022
Join our WordFire Press Readers Group for
sneak previews, updates, new projects, and giveaways.
Sign up at wordfirepress.com

CONTENTS

INTRODUCTION

I am no stranger to rejection—and I don't just mean my various attempts to get a date for prom in high school. I vividly remember the day I got my first rejection slip for a story I had submitted to a magazine.

I was twelve years old.

I'd always wanted to be a writer, and I spent every second of free time in my bedroom at an electric typewriter, pounding out drafts of a science fiction novel I'd been writing since third grade. As a Christmas present one year, my parents got me a subscription to *Writer's Digest* magazine, and I learned all about manuscript format, markets, and the submission process. I bought a copy of *Writer's Market*, a big fat directory of magazine markets and their submission guidelines.

As a freshman in high school, I wrote a short story for history class about young twin boys trying to survive the Black Death in the 14th Century. I thought it was pretty good, and it got an "A" in history class, so I screwed up my courage, typed a clean copy, and mailed it to *Boys' Life* magazine, which seemed the appropriate market. I included a stamped, self-addressed return envelope, added a polite cover letter, and dropped it in the mailbox with a silent prayer. Then I waited ... nearly three months.

I went to the mailbox every day, hoping and hoping, until finally the manila envelope came back. My heart fell. I tore open the envelope. Clipped to the front of the manuscript was a printed form rejection slip: "Dear Author, We regret that your story does not meet our needs at this time. Please try again." Cold and generic.

I was devastated. All that work, all that waiting—for nothing more than a rejection!

It was the first of many.

Undaunted, I resolved to try again and again—not just with the Black Death story, but with new stories. I would polish each one, make myself better, improve my writing. I vowed that I would get something published.

I combed through the *Writer's Market*, found magazines that might be appropriate for my stories. I developed an index-card recordkeeping system in a recipe box to keep track of where I had submitted my stories and which markets had rejected them.

I collected 80 rejection slips before I got my first acceptance—a one-page flash-fiction story that was published in a Wisconsin high school writings magazine. I received no pay, only a couple of contributor copies. I was a junior in high school.

A year later I finally sold a short story *for pay*—$12.50—to a small press magazine, *Space and Time*. I was thrilled! I could finally say I had been paid for my fiction.

Seeing the dollar amount, my parents were not overly

impressed. It didn't come close to reimbursing even the postage I had invested so far. But it was a start.

I kept collecting rejection slips, hundreds and hundreds of them. Now, in retrospect, I can see that most of those early works weren't worthy of publication anyway. But my writing, plotting, characters, and descriptions improved. Practice makes perfect. I studied writing. I read voraciously. I tried to get better and better and better. Those form rejection slips were frequently replaced with personal letters, words of encouragement, suggestions for improvement.

I came close, so close ... but not quite.

When I was a senior in high school, age seventeen, I received a particularly encouraging, detailed letter from Dr. Stanley Schmidt, the editor of *Analog* magazine—the holy grail for science fiction writers.

October 15, 1979
Dear Mr. Anderson:

Thank you for letting me see UPON THE WINDS. It had an intriguingly imaginative idea behind it, and I think the telling shows a good deal of potential. Your ability to visualize an exotic setting, and enable the reader to do so too, is quite good. However, your skills do need some honing (which is hardly surprising); a good deal of that should come with practice, but sometimes the process is speeded by pointing out where some of the needs are. In style, the first thing I notice is that you have a tendency to lean rather heavily on long, lecture-like explanations of background: in general, it's better to get right into the action and reveal background gradually and as unobtrusively as possible. It's hard with a story like this, where there's a good deal that has to be established right at the outset, but it can be done and needs to be done.

The other thing is a matter of a special set of science-fictional skills, which are always helpful, but for Analog they're essential. You have to make sure your exotic setting works. I don't think this one does; the picture I get here is of the Noreed living in isolation on an otherwise essentially lifeless world. This won't work; an animal functions only as part of an interlocking ecosystem which, at the very least, must also include some plants (or things that serve the ecological functions of plants). What I'd recommend doing is backing all the way up to the formation of this planet and thinking out how it evolved and life evolved on it. The process will almost certainly lead to a richer ecology and fuller understanding of why the Noreed act as they do — which may turn out, inevitably, to be significantly different from the way you've pictured it here. But it will be a more believable way, because the reader will sense that what you tell him is part of a self-consistent larger whole, even if most of the supporting detail never finds its way into the final story. This is one of the most important "secrets" of writing successful science fiction about alien worlds. I don't know how much you know about the astronomical and biological thinking that's needed to do this sort of thing, but there's a basic body of it which is so important that you should familiarize yourself with it as soon as possible if you're seriously interested in writing science fiction; the time will be well invested, and I think you'll enjoy it. A few readings you should try, if you haven't already done so, are these: the two essays on creating imaginary worlds and beings by Poul

*Anderson and Hal Clement, in Reginald Bretnor's book
SCIENCE FICTION: TODAY AND TOMORROW; I.S.
Shklovskii and Carl Sagan's INTELLIGENT LIFE IN
THE UNIVERSE; and Poul Anderson's IS THERE LIFE
ON OTHER WORLDS? and Stephen H. Dole's HABIT-
ABLE PLANETS FOR MAN. I think you'll find these not
only help you learn to create solid settings, but are just
bristling with good story ideas.*

*Meanwhile, keep writing, and I'll look forward to seeing
your future work.*

*Sincerely,
Stanley Schmidt
Editor*

That rejection meant the world to me—this was the
biggest editor in my field! It was one of the best things to
happen to me as a young writer. I was energized and determined, and eventually (many years later) I did publish a
story in *Analog*, and then several more. I became good
friends with Stan.

I went to writing conferences, entered contests, and
even won my first award as a writer ... although it was a
dubious honor, at best. At a large writing conference I
received a trophy—engraved brass plaque and everything—
naming me "The Writer with No Future," because I could
produce more rejection slips *by weight* than any other
writer at the entire conference. Though it was meant to be a
joke, I took the trophy as a badge of honor, and it only
increased my determination. I would not give up.

The happy ending is that I did rise to the top of the slushpile. I have now published over 150 short stories and 170 novels, many of which became international bestsellers. I have 23 million copies in print in more than 30 languages —so I don't let the rejections get me down.

My friend and mentor, Dean Koontz, once said that a writer's first million words are just practice ... and if you can get paid for your practice, that's great. But you are not wasting your time. You are learning your trade.

———————

This book will give you a look behind the scenes at how the slushpile for a magazine or anthology works. I'll give you tips on how to cope with rejection and, more importantly, how to avoid it in the first place.

I hope it'll help you get out of the reject pile and into print.

THE SLUSHPILE

S ubmitting an unsolicited work to a magazine used to be called "sending a story over the transom." A transom is the narrow window above a door, often left open for air circulation. Apparently, writers used to toss their submissions through the open window above a publisher's door so they would land on an editor's desk.

It doesn't happen that way anymore, but is still an appropriate metaphor for how authors throw their precious stories into the great black hole of the editorial slushpile, a vast swamp of unread manuscripts, all of them crying out for attention, desperate to be chosen.

An "unsolicited submission" is a story that an author blindly sends in. No editor has requested it, no one at the publication is expecting it. Write your best story, throw it over the transom, and take your chances.

A "solicited story," on the other hand, has been specifically requested by the editor, whether on a certain topic or because they want something by a particular author. A solicited manuscript pretty much has a guaranteed acceptance, unless the author does such a horrible job there's simply no recourse but to reject it. Keep in mind, though, that any *solicited* author will be a professional and can be counted on to deliver good work.

As a new author, I studied the market listings and learned the names of the editors, who seemed like the gods of Olympus to me. With the fate of so many aspiring writers in their hands, these couldn't possibly be mere human beings! When I submitted to a large magazine, I imagined that dump trucks delivered mountains of manuscripts to an immense warehouse like the one that held the Ark of the Covenant. What chance did my story possibly have of being noticed among all those millions?

And yet I kept trying.

Later, I was astonished to learn that my mentor, Stan Schmidt of *Analog* magazine, had a habit of reclining in the hammock in his backyard and reading manuscript after manuscript. The more I got to know other writers, editors, and publishers, the more I began to realize that my preconceptions were as much fiction as my stories.

The submission process took on an entirely different perspective when I saw it from the opposite side of the slushpile.

One of my closest friends, Kristine Kathryn Rusch, was the editor of *The Magazine of Fantasy & Science Fiction*, one of the largest publications in the field. During a visit with Kris and her husband, Dean Wesley Smith, my wife and I spent an eye-opening day helping sift through the magazine submissions.

Yes, this story is about a bygone day when people actually sent paper manuscripts through the actual mail in envelopes with stamps on them. Today, I can't imagine submitting to a market that doesn't accept electronic submissions. (And as an editor myself, I can't conceive of working with an author who couldn't provide an electronic file!) Nevertheless, the consideration process is the same.

Dean returned from the post office with the day's mail, two large bins packed with envelopes. He dumped everything in the middle of the living room floor, and the four of us got to work.

Initially, we culled out the regular letters, simple requests for guidelines, inquiries about submitted manuscripts or subscription copies.

Once those were gone, Kris went through the large pile of manila envelopes, each of which contained a hopeful writer's manuscript. Like a blackjack dealer with a deck of cards, Kris flipped through the stack, keeping her eye on the return address and the submitter's name, piling up the manuscripts. Occasionally, she would extract one and place it on a separate, much smaller stack. These were submissions from authors whose names she recognized, not only well-known writers but promising new ones who had come very close in the past. These stories, she explained, had the best chance of being accepted. She would read them herself.

Then Dean, my wife, and I considered the remaining manuscripts, about 90 percent of the original stack. We opened the envelopes one at a time. Any submitted story without a stamped, self-addressed reply envelope was immediately tossed out. That seemed cold-hearted to me at first—but why should the editor have to pay postage for an author who couldn't read the instructions? Those stories literally went in the wastebasket without a second thought.

Next we rejected any story that wasn't in standard manuscript format. If the writer couldn't follow basic formatting rules—which were clearly stated in the maga-zine's guidelines and in a thousand other writers' resources —then their work simply wasn't worth considering. Any submission printed on pink paper, or in unreadable dot matrix letters, or a dog-eared, coffee-stained manuscript was just stuffed in the return envelope and summarily rejected. (Granted, this is different with electronic submissions, but the formatting conditions are still vital.)

Third, we looked at the cover letters. Any submitter who identified the enclosed story as previously published was also summarily rejected, since *F&SF* was only looking for original work.

One cover letter said, "If you don't publish my story, I'll track you down and kill you, bitch!" That one not only got rejected, but the cover letter was also filed in the "crazy person" file—which I learned was distressingly thick.

After those steps, we had cut the mountain of submis-sions in half, but there were still many dozens remaining. So, the three of us divided the pile and got to reading. Our task, according to Kris, was to go through all these unso-licited submissions and find one—yes, only one!—that we thought was worth her time to read.

Honestly, it was tough to find one.

The stories eliminated in these first stages got a preprinted form rejection slip. "Thank you. Please try again." But any story that made it to the final consideration, read by the editor herself, received a genuine personal note, usually with comments or at least some note of encouragement.

And that was just the mail from one day. *F&SF* received the same number of submissions the next day, and the next —every single day.

And all those slushpile submissions competed against tales sent in by well-known, big-name, or award-winning writers.

Out of which the editor could select maybe five stories a month.

Do the math.

———————

THE *F&SF* slushpile experience taught me many things. Not only did it give me a surprising and realistic view of the submission and consideration process, but it also made me recognize numerous things a writer could do to increase their odds, how they could get their work to be considered by the main editor instead of some flunky first reader (like me).

It shocked me that many of those factors had nothing to do with the brilliance of the prose or the originality of the story. By using simple courtesy, professionalism, and common sense, you could jump through those hoops and get into the finalist pile.

This book will teach you how to do that.

2

THE EDITOR'S PERSPECTIVE

As an aspiring, optimistic, and persistent writer, I had a blind spot. Each time I hurled a manuscript at that towering wall, I thought only about how I could make the all-powerful editor choose my story over all the others. I never stopped to think what that slushpile mountain looked like from the editor's side.

Imagine yourself facing that never-ending avalanche of fiction. Each day, the mail brings another load—and you have to process them all, at least filter out the deadwood, before the next day's avalanche comes. And the next day's. They never stop, not for weekends, not for holidays. Sure, an editor could take a day off, but that just meant twice as many manuscripts to read the following day.

I have edited thirteen anthologies to date, including the three bestselling science fiction anthologies of all time. Some of these books were only open to invited authors, and I didn't consider any outside submissions. In those cases, the stories came in a steady, easily manageable stream.

My three *Blood Lite* anthologies were put together

7

under the auspices of the Horror Writers Association, a professional organization, open only to members of HWA— a large pool, but a limited one. That produced a curling whitecap wave of submissions, but I could keep up with them all.

But some of my anthologies were completely open to the general public, with professional pay rates—and that was like a tsunami.

I RUN the Publishing Masters Degree program at Western Colorado University. For their primary thesis project, my graduate students create, solicit, and edit an original anthology. Thanks to a grant from Draft2Digital, we pay professional rates, and submissions are open to the general public.

The students have no idea what they're in for.

After they write the anthology description and call for submissions, they ambitiously post the notice everywhere and spread the word far and wide in order to get the very best stories. I warn them that it'll be a flood, but they are earnest and energetic.

Then the submissions start coming in.

Oh, the students start out vowing to do right by the authors. They tell themselves they're going to read every manuscript, give it due and careful consideration. To prepare them, I insist that they don't have to read every submission through to the end. Within the first page or so, they'll have a feel for the prose quality and will know pretty quickly whether or not a particular story has a chance of making it. But no matter how much I insist, they are determined to read every single story.

It usually takes them about a week to get over it.

After the first few days of sorting stories, one student wrote me, "Whoa, you weren't kidding. Most of these are terrible! Sometimes you can tell just by looking at the cover letter."

Diana Gill, a former editor for HarperCollins, once said in a conference talk, "I am not required to read every submission all the way through. My obligation as an editor is to choose the very best stories and produce the best book that readers will enjoy. Think about it: My *job* is to go through these stories. If you can't hold the interest of someone who's *getting paid* to read them, then you certainly won't hold the interest of someone just looking for a good read."

So FAR MY students have produced two anthologies, *Monsters, Movies & Mayhem*, and *Unmasked*. For *MM&M* they received over 300 submissions; for *Unmasked* they sorted through 535.

For the first book, the editorial team managed the slushpile through brute force, creating their own spreadsheet, logging the arrivals each day by hand. As the nine people plowed through the manuscripts, they maintained their own score sheet, rating each story as Yes, No, or Maybe. After the submissions closed and the doors slammed shut, we collated the scores, and decided to get rid of all but the top fifty or so stories. The students wrote the first round of rejection slips, then they debated over the remaining submissions, choosing the very best ones and working within our budgeted word count.

For the second anthology, we used an application called Moksha, a portal and submissions-management app that took care of the onerous recordkeeping. Moksha requires the submitting authors to input most of the metadata—the title, word count, and email address for response. If an author tries to submit something longer than the maximum word count allowed, they are automatically blocked. This takes the tedious recordkeeping—and potential for error—out of the hands of the editorial board.

Another more complicated, more broad-based, and much more expensive submissions-management application is called Submittable, which some big publishers use; but Moksha served our needs just fine. With Moksha, each member of the editorial team could mark whether or not they had read a submission, score it, and leave comments (which are not viewable by anyone but the executive editor, me, until I decide to release them). Moksha was a huge help when we received nearly twice as many submissions for *Unmasked* as for *MM&M*.

The students were stunned when nearly a hundred manuscripts were received in the final week, as people had waited until the last minute to submit their stories. During that daunting surge, the students had to assess and weed out all but the top contenders at breakneck speed.

Yes, there was a lot of stress and consternation.

When legendary writer, editor, reviewer, and writing instructor Algis Budrys workshopped stories among his students, he taught a concept called the "Budrys Line."

When considering each manuscript, Budrys would put on his editor hat and hardliner attitude, and he drew a bold, red line across the page at the point where he stopped reading. This was where the slushpile manuscript earned a rejection.

Sometimes (much to the writer's dismay) the Budrys Line occurred at the bottom of the first page, or the first paragraph, or even the first line. His writing students would wail to him, "But it pays off in the end! You have to see the twist on the last page!" Or, "But I need to do character setup or scene setting."

Doesn't matter. If the reader isn't hooked by that first page, all your development or clever twists later on will be for naught, because no one will get there. Don't waste your time on literary dithering. Your job as an author is to move that Budrys Line all the way to the last sentence on the last page.

Hearing Budrys lecture on this, I had an epiphany in understanding the editor's perspective:

The editor is not looking for any reason to keep going.

The editor is trying to find any excuse to stop and move on to the next manuscript in the pile.

Don't give the editor that excuse.

In the following chapters I will present tips on how to move that Budrys Line; how to get the overburdened and jaded editor to actually read your story.

After that, it's up to you.

3

BE PROFESSIONAL AND COURTEOUS

When you submit to a market, you are not just sending in your story—you're auditioning for a job. You're showing the editor what kind of writer you'll be to work with on a professional level.

Don't be a jerk.

Most editors are pragmatic. It's not worth publishing the most brilliant piece of fiction in the world if the author will be an absolute nightmare. Life is too short.

Remember the author who submitted to *F&SF* with the cover letter, "If you don't publish my story, I'll track you down and kill you, bitch!" Even if that piece was the next Pulitzer Prize winner, Nebula winner, Hugo winner, or anything else, the editor wouldn't touch him with a ten-foot rejection slip. (And with an author attitude like that, I'm certain the story was a piece of crap as well.)

For *Unmasked*, one person sent in a badly written, clunky story that didn't even make the first cut. One of the editors rejected it with a basic, bland form letter, and the writer responded with the following:

"I don't even remember trying to place it with you. You know if it were a few decades back you might have been interested in an author gaybashing a few gay characters. You know how good gay bashing was in that Jack Nicholson movie 'As Good As It Gets?' But the media now-a-days is selling gay shit to everyone as if they are about love. No, gay people are not about love. They are the most toxic, sick, twisted, bastard race to ever walk the Earth. You know what they say, God created Adam and Eve, and then the Devil came said, 'Hi, I'm Steve!' Once you get to know a few good gay characters, you'll know all of those bastards descended from the Devil!

And no, I am not religious. F**k your God!

Kind regards,

[author]"

So, uh, in what conceivable universe would we ever want to work with that person?

SOME EDITORS and writers debate whether cover letters are even necessary. What is the author going to say? "I've sent this story for your consideration." Duh!

For my own part, I like a cover letter when it has something to say. If you've got significant writing credits, be sure to list them because I'm not likely to recognize every name.

If you've met me personally, or if you've attended one of my workshops, or if you've talked with me at a convention, remind me of that. "I met you at Clothesline Convention in Oklahoma City, and we talked about Prog rock music." That won't necessarily increase your chances of acceptance if your story isn't any good, but it will put a face to a name, and I'll likely at least read your submission (well, unless you acted like an ass when we met).

If you have specialized knowledge that's relevant to the submission, mention that. If your story is about spending the night in a hospital morgue, and you once spent a summer as a morgue attendant, then tell me that. Even if you have a life detail that's just plain interesting—that you've twice won the Iditarod sled race across Alaska, for example—include that, because it makes you a *person*, rather than just an anonymous manuscript.

Above all, be professional. Be courteous. Be someone that the editor can be comfortable working with.

———

Lisa Mangum, editor for Shadow Mountain Books, sent me the following, and very appropriate rant:

Pro Tip from the Slushpile: "How Not to Be a Jerk" Edition. Yet another response to a rejection letter saying that I'm "rude" and "thoughtless," and it would "only take a few minutes to share 1 or 2 sentences of honest feedback as to why the manuscript was rejected."

sigh

If I, in a given year, reject 3000 submissions (ballpark for easy math), and if I spent 60 seconds to write one line about why the manuscript was rejected, that would be 50 hours of time I don't have.

Besides, if I only have one minute to tell you—honestly, per this woman's demand—why your book is being rejected, it's going to end up being something like, "The writing is poor, and the characters are underdeveloped." Or perhaps, "I don't know why I don't like it—I just don't." Or even, "I've seen this idea a million times before; you didn't do anything to make it unique."

Not sure that is kinder or a more thoughtful way to say simply, "We decided not to publish your manuscript."

I bumped into another editor online once who said it this way: "Pretend you are applying for a job at McDonald's. You send in your resume. So do 50 other people. Maybe you get an interview. So do 30 other people. The answer, however, is no.

"Do you then ask the HR manager to give you detailed feedback on what you did wrong? Why they chose someone else over you? Or perhaps do you then request that they tell you where you might go to find another job? Or even demand that they spend their spare time actually finding you another job?"

No. You don't. You say, "Thank you for your time," and you keep looking for another job.

So, Nice Lady Who Thinks I'm Rude and Mean, go ahead and "work with one of [my] competitors." That's not the threat you think it is.

After all, if you've got a publishing deal lined up else-where, great. But why bother telling me that you're mad I didn't give you feedback on your manuscript?

———

THE EDITOR of a major science fiction magazine posted this forehead-slapper on social media. (Warning, some of the language is offensive ... but really funny.)

. . .

"I GET many replies to the rejections I write for [magazine], with numerous thank-yous, which are unnecessary, and lots of requests for additional feedback, which I can't provide. But every so often I get a response like this one, which I received today.

Don't say unfortunately,!!! and if my story didn't win you over, let me tell you something you are not my GOD, and if you are going to pass my story to your stupid magazine what they call Fantasy and science fiction, you stupid ugly Mother f**ker. Motherf**ker don't wish me anything I didn't tell you to advise me, well there are many things in the world and you and your stupid magazine is not the end.

I wish you to go to hell and find the best of luck finding the right market for it you Motherf**ker stupid."

It's often at times like these that I consider changing my basic form letters from something that might be encouraging or perhaps helpful to this:

"Dear Writer,
No.
Sincerely,
etc."

I considered saying "No thanks" but who knows how that might be misinterpreted or any of the ways it might set someone off!

You CAN'T MAKE this stuff up.

Let's just say as a predominant rule, don't respond to rejections, no matter how politely. Just don't. What do you expect to accomplish? Act like a professional, and you'll be treated like a professional.

4

TRICKS DON'T WORK

K nowing the extent of the competition against you—all those unsolicited stories sent in over the transom!—you might want to pull out a few little tricks to increase your odds, to make your story stand out.

Don't.

Seasoned editors have seen every trick, and they won't be fooled.

If you're sending in a hardcopy manuscript, don't clip a $20 bill to the first page. Don't send chocolates, especially if your package will sit in a hot mail room. Don't send the editor an Amazon or Starbucks gift card as a "special thanks, in advance of reading my story."

These things may make your submission stand out all right, but not in the way you want the editor to notice you. You'll look like a creep and an amateur.

Don't format your manuscript with a fancy, scrolly font for a fantasy piece, or a high-tech science fiction font for a space opera. Editors will hate it. See the next chapter on proper manuscript format.

Don't assume the editor is forgetful, or just plain stupid.

When I began editing my first *Blood Lite* anthology, I received a submission about a kid feeding radioactive food to a packet of sea monkeys, which then grew into monsters that broke out of their tank and killed the family. The story was okay, but it didn't make the cut, so I rejected it.

The following year, when I edited *Blood Lite II*, I received another submission about a kid feeding radioactive food to a packet of sea monkeys, which then grew into monsters that broke out of their tank and killed the family. I didn't remember the author, but I certainly remembered the story. It still didn't work for me, so I rejected it again. I didn't offer any particular encouragement, and I was a little annoyed that he had sent the same story.

The following year I edited *Blood Lite III* and—you guessed it—the same story came back around. This time I didn't hold back when I responded: "I didn't like this story the first time I rejected it. I liked it even less the second time you sent it. And I certainly won't be accepting it the third time. Please do not submit again."

We remember things like that. Don't get on the editor's poop list.

5
FOLLOW STANDARD MANUSCRIPT FORMAT

Standard manuscript format is called "standard" for a reason. That is exactly the format an editor expects. This is one of the easiest ways to improve your odds and step ahead of the rank amateurs.

In a stack of hundreds of other contenders, you *don't* want your story to stand out because you can't follow the simplest, most basic template.

While we were reviewing submissions for *Unmasked* and *Monsters, Movies & Mayhem*, the editorial board would automatically reject any story not in proper format. Period. It was an easy way to sift out the rank amateurs.

One indignant author, after receiving his rejection for exactly that reason, wrote, "How am I supposed to know what standard manuscript format is?"

Seriously? If you can't figure that one out, then you'll never overcome the far more difficult obstacles ahead of you in your writing career. Google "standard manuscript format" for plenty of examples. Countless writing manuals and magazines give extensive guidelines. If you're too lazy to do that, please don't submit to any of my markets.

Okay, *sigh*, I'll put it here, too. Your document should be double-spaced and in a standard font—preferably Courier or Times New Roman—with one-inch margins all around, right and left, top and bottom.

On the first page include the title and your author name. In the upper left corner include your name, pen name if any, email and physical mailing address. Yes, most business will be done electronically, but we do need a physical address to send your contributor copies when it's published.

In the upper right corner put the word count. Yes, the editor can always open the file and run a word count, but when we're putting an anthology or magazine together, or arranging the order of stories in the table of contents, we want a quick way to refer to the story length without going through the hassle. Make life easier for your editors. Put all that information right there on the first page.

Include a header on top of every page with your name, story title and page number. Why? If it's an electronic manuscript, what does it matter?

Because some editors still like to print and read in hard copy, maybe in a hammock in their backyard or relaxing in the bathtub or at a campsite in the woods.

It doesn't matter. You don't need the reasons why. *Just do it*.

An author simply has no excuse not to get this part right, because it takes zero talent. Just follow instructions. Why risk having your story rejected outright because you can't apply some basic formatting rules?

One more note about getting "cute" with formatting or fonts.

Sometimes there's a creative reason in your story to break these rules. You might think it's interesting to use a wonky font for the dialogue of an alien, for example, or a high-tech font for computer screens ... or a newspaper font to indicate clippings.

Yes, your creative writing class or your critique group applauded you for being innovative and clever. I still advise against it. You don't know the production capabilities or the design team of your publication. Magazines or book publishers have standard templates for their layouts. They use book-design software packages that may have varying degrees of flexibility.

At WordFire Press, we use a powerful layout application called Vellum, which does just about everything we need. Even so, Vellum has some frustrating limitations in our ability to add unusual fonts midstream, or to format sections outside of the basic template.

One story submitted to *Monsters, Movies & Mayhem* was about an actor becoming so obsessed with his role that he evolved into the character; in the manuscript, the formatting gradually shifted from standard prose to very specialized movie-script format. The story itself was quite good, and we held it for the final round of decisions, but when I took one look at the manuscript formatting, I vetoed it. The sheer, daunting task of reproducing that layout in the final publication would be more work than the rest of the book combined. When writing that story, I'm sure the author never gave a thought to the publisher's design and layout flexibility.

WHEN I ASKED the anthology board to write up their impressions after the lengthy editorial process, here are some of their comments regarding manuscript format:

1) Some readers want to print before reading. This means Author's name or title and a page number in the header makes things a lot easier to keep the reader on course in your story.

2) In the submission form, a few authors screwed up their own email address. That means, unless you put your contact info correctly in the manuscript, there might be NO WAY TO REACH YOU. Which is just silly. Don't make me Google you to give you good news.

3) Lines between paragraphs, different fonts and sizes, margin differences, etc. can show up in VASTLY different ways, depending on the hardware and software where it is viewed. So, though you might not like Times New Roman, understand that it is the standard not because it looks good, but because it's UNIVERSALLY INSTALLED. Your readers might be using anything from a printer, to a mobile phone, to an ebook reader, from word-to-pdf converter to Google doc previewer. If you think you know exactly what your manuscript looks like, think again.

4) It shows that you read the guidelines and cared about my (the reader's) time. So, if I have time to read only one story before bed, don't give me a reason to think yours isn't a good bet.

5) While you're formatting, you are taking another look at your text from a critical viewpoint, which gives you another chance to spot spelling, punctuation, or other errors, especially near the beginning where they cause the most damage to your first impression.

6) As previously mentioned, when push came to shove and deadlines loomed, it provided an easy hurdle to disqualify stories when there just wasn't time to read every single one.

7) Finally, it displays a knowledge of professional standards and experience in submitting. This in turn communicates things about what it will be like to work with you.

We had over 500 submissions come in. Why would I want to reformat each one before I read it, even if it only takes a minute, when we gave utterly clear guidelines and even provided a sample? (And it's *standard* format, that all writers should know and follow; not some odd quirk that I was asking for.) And when I want to grab a dozen, print them out so I can take them with me away for a weekend, I don't want to go into each one and change or add their headers because the authors couldn't add their name and page number on the top.

Imagine you're getting 1,500 submissions per month, and 1,400 require a few commands each to change font and spacing. It seems small when it's one manuscript, but the hassle factor adds up. So it's good to be a no-hassle author.

When I just spent an afternoon working on payments and contracts for the 21 authors, four of them didn't bother to put their word count or address/contact information on the front page. That caused me problems, because then I had to do several steps of extra work, digging through emails or referring back to the contracts. I don't WANT to do extra work, dozens if not hundreds of times, even if it doesn't seem like a big deal to somebody else. Make sense?

—————

THERE IS power in being easy to work with, and conforming to the style guidelines is a sign that you're easy to work with.

Just do it. No excuses.

6

SEND IN A CLEAN MANUSCRIPT

Everybody makes mistakes, but you're not allowed to—at least, not here. Make sure your manuscript is clean, with no misspellings, typos, incorrect punctuation, or sloppy grammar.

Run a spellcheck! Proofread it, then have someone else proofread it, because you won't catch everything yourself.

Some small glitch may slip through, or you might miss a genuine typo, but when I'm digging through a tall stack of submissions, and your story has a glaring spelling mistake or clunky grammar on the very first page, I'll assume your story is going to be sloppy all the way through.

As with the previous chapter, this one is a no-brainer. Take the time. Send in a clean manuscript, and you'll leave another part of the slushpile in the dust.

7

FOLLOW THE GUIDELINES

Before you submit to a market, read the guidelines. Don't assume they're all the same. Every publication has specific needs, restrictions, length limitations, submission periods, and most importantly, subject matter.

For *Unmasked*, we wrote up detailed guidelines, slaved over the perfect description of our concept, stated clearly what we were looking for, listed the length limitations, specified no previously published stories and no simultaneous submissions.

Of the 535 submissions we received in the slushpile, about 400 of them ignored the guidelines.

Our anthologies had a specific submission period—usually September 1 through October 31.

Don't submit to us before we're open. We won't even look at it.

Don't send us a story after the deadline closes. We won't even look at it. (Fortunately, Moksha automatically blocks anything outside of the open submission window.)

Check the length guidelines. Some editors are a little more flexible on this, while others have a hard-and-fast rule. When in doubt, you can always query the editor. "I've got a story that's 300 words over your length limit. Is this a hard rule, or can I still submit?" Maybe they'll be flexible; maybe they won't.

For my recent anthologies, we had a specific cap of 5,000 words—not 10,000, not 6,000, not 5,001. That may seem a little arbitrary, but when the editorial team is faced with many hundreds of submissions, that's just one more filtering mechanism. Can the author follow simple instructions?

———

NEXT, send the right sort of thing. If the market is looking for short fiction, then ... uh, send *short fiction*. Not limericks. Not non-fiction essays. Not Christmas memoirs.

For *Unmasked*, we wanted stories that had something to do with masks and unmasking, and we were open to a range of genres, from science fiction, to fantasy, horror, or thrillers.

One person submitted an actual college term paper about how Beethoven wore a mask when writing one of his works (it even had the college course number and the professor's name on it). We rejected the story, saying we weren't looking for non-fiction. A week later, it came over the transom again—the exact same paper, but with a different author name attached (although the professor and course number were still there on the first page). It got rejected again.

At least it wasn't about sea monkeys ...

In one case, somebody submitted six pieces of Christmas art. Baffled, I rejected that one out of hand with a brief, polite note, "Please carefully read the guidelines before submitting to any market." The author responded by sending me a discount coupon to a Carson City, NV, brothel. (You can't make this stuff up.)

Previously Unpublished Stories Only.

It means just what it says—we don't want a story that's been published elsewhere. There's nothing wrong with reprints, and many markets will allow them, but check the guidelines. For our anthologies, we wanted only original work.

Someone submitted a story that the editorial team rather liked, making no mention that the piece was a reprint. One diligent student, however, took the initiative to run an internet search and discovered the story for sale as a standalone ebook and also an audio story. The submitter hadn't bothered to inform us.

Instant REJECT.

No simultaneous submissions.

If you're going to submit to our market, you need to give us a chance to look at it exclusively. We respond quickly enough; just wait for it. For each anthology, we look at a lot of manuscripts, and we made our decisions within a month of the closing date. Please don't send it elsewhere in the meantime.

For *Unmasked*, many of the editors liked one particular story, so it went into the second tier. Every editor read it for that round, and it again made the next cut. We all read a third time, then spent hours on a conference call comparing our favorite picks, arguing, horse-trading. That story made the final cut; we wanted to put it into the anthology. We sent a happy acceptance letter to all of the winners, and then rejected all the others. We had constructed our anthology, right within our word count and budget.

Then the author responded, "Oh, I sent it elsewhere and sold it to another market in the meantime. Sorry."

I was furious. Our guidelines clearly stated No Simultaneous Submissions. That's like offering an engagement ring to your partner, only to find out that they've been dating all over the place and got pregnant by someone else.

This writer had wasted my time and everyone else's time. Not only that, we had already rejected the other contenders, one of which would have taken the slot in the anthology, so now we had lost all of our second choices, too.

It was truly inconsiderate and unprofessional behavior, and I would never work with that author again.

8

FOLLOW THE GUIDELINES!

Don't send a magic elf story to *Analog*, a strict hard-SF magazine.

Don't send graphic horror or erotica to *Boys' Life* magazine.

I can tell you're rolling your eyes because it's so painfully obvious. Alas, it's not all that obvious.

Read the guidelines and send the editor something close to what they're looking for. If you expect the editor to take the time to read your manuscript, then make a little effort yourself and research what the market is looking for. Read issues of the magazine, if possible, so you can understand the editor's tastes. Would you go into an important job interview unprepared?

Sometimes, a publication's guidelines are intentionally broad—general science fiction, for example, or fantasy ranging from modern urban fantasy to epic high fantasy. That means you have a lot of leeway. Other times, the guidelines are excruciatingly specific.

I once helped edit an anthology of stories about purple

unicorns—that's pretty narrow. Another oddball anthology from many years ago contained stories about Carmen Miranda's ghost haunting a space station. I once contributed a story to an anthology in which every single story opened with the line "There were rats in the soufflé again." (And it was the *second volume* of such stories!)

I EDITED three *Blood Lite* anthologies for the Horror Writers Association. My guidelines were fairly broad—humorous horror stories. In other words, horror stories that were also funny. I was willing to look at all kinds of submissions. My definition of "horror" was pretty broad. The tales could be psychological suspense or classic monster stories, but they also had to make me laugh ... or at least try to. Submissions were only open to members of HWA, a professional organization, so presumably all writers had at least a few pro credits.

I received one story that opened with a serial killer raping and murdering a college coed. He gloated about it, raped and murdered a second coed, almost got caught but managed to escape, then in the end, he did it a third time and got away, planning to kill more.

The end.

As I read through the horrific descriptions, which were well-enough written, I kept trying to figure out how was this ever going to be *funny*? I read page after page, and as the gore and violence escalated, I kept thinking "This better have a heck of a punchline!"

It didn't. There was nothing anyone could even remotely construe as humorous.

I was so baffled that when I rejected the piece, I wrote the author asking what in the world he thought might be funny about that story? Why did he feel it was appropriate for *Blood Lite*? The author responded that he didn't have any other story to send, so he just decided to give it a shot.

This was really annoying. Not only was this submission never, ever going to make it into *Blood Lite*, the author had *wasted my time*! When looking at the stack of manuscripts I had to go through, most of them from authors who had done their homework and genuinely tried to give me an appropriate story, this person had disrespected my time and my patience.

That is not the way you want an editor to remember your name.

9

FOLLOW THE DAMN GUIDELINES!!!

See Chapters 7 and 8.

10

DON'T WAIT UNTIL THE LAST MINUTE

I f an anthology has a specific submission period and a deadline, don't wait until the end to send your submission in.

Yes, you technically have until midnight on the very last day, but in reality most writers also hold off until the last minute, and your story will be lost in the stampede. On the other hand, if you send your story in early, you have less competition and a less frazzled editorial staff. They'll be patient and eager to give your work a chance, and they'll give it more consideration.

For *Unmasked* we received a hundred of the 535 submissions in the last week. By then, the editors were already harried and burned out. As the flood of stories increased, they had less and less patience for even the most minor infractions. Had those submissions come in a month earlier, the stories would have received a far more thorough consideration.

Sometimes you have no choice but to use the full time

available. You really and truly need to polish your story right up until the deadline.

But if you can get it in ahead of the last dash, the odds will be more in your favor.

11

WRITE A GOOD STORY

As I compile these chapters, every piece of advice seems so obvious that it shouldn't need to be said. That's even more true for this one.

The previous tips in this book will help you move closer to the front of the line. By following that advice, you can avoid mistakes that will get you rejected outright. But once your manuscript actually gets its moment in the spotlight, when your words are before the eyes of the editor—then it's up to you.

There are countless books, workshops, seminars, and classes on how to set the hook, describe the setting, develop your characters, build your world, work out an intricate plot, write active prose, use vivid descriptions.

That is beyond the scope of this book.

The advice is simple. Write a great story with compelling characters, vivid writing, a unique idea, great plot, powerful emotions, and sparkling prose. That part is up to you.

Remember the Algis Budrys Line—Don't give the editor any reason to stop. Make your manuscript great all the way through. The way to get your story accepted is simply by being better than the competition.

See? Simple and straightforward.

12

SLUSHPILE MEMORIES—
FROM THE STUDENT EDITORS

W hen I decided to put together this book, I asked my students to write down their slush-pile memories and offer advice after battling the flood of submissions. What did they learn from the slushpile, and what advice would they pass on to other authors?

Many said the same thing, over and over again. Even though it may seem redundant, I'm including all those comments to emphasize the magnitude of the mistakes encountered, the frustrations they repeatedly felt.

I hope that reading these accounts will hammer the lesson home.

READ THE GUIDELINES. This is by far the most important advice you can get. If it helps, copy and paste the guidelines into another document, and separate the sentences into individual instructions, so you can make a checklist and be sure you got all the details. We didn't put any details in there by accident.

One quick example: our guidelines asked for submissions in proper manuscript format, and we even gave a link so they could look at a manuscript and review what the format included. ALMOST EVERYONE ignored this, even pro writers who should know better. Did we reject on that basis? Well, not at the beginning, but towards the end when we had a huge pile of slush and one week to finish reading, we were looking for excuses to reject, and many, many stories were axed for not being in manuscript format. Were some of those great, publishable stories? Almost certainly. We'll never know for sure, though.

Tons more were rejected for submitting previously published stories, or being over the word count, even by one word. All because they broke the requirements we clearly covered in the guidelines.

SUBMIT EARLY. Even though we had a two-month window, the stories we received in the first two weeks got the freshest eyes and the most consideration. We had a rating system of 1–10, and there were 1s and 2s that I read to completion in the first couple of weeks, but that did not happen as we neared the end. I graded much higher at the beginning as well. Readers who are in a hurry to finish are looking for excuses to reject, so get them your work before they're in a hurry.

. . .

FULLY INCORPORATE THE THEME, if there is one. Our anthology's theme was "Unmasked," and we had a number of people write GREAT stories, but which made us in the end ask "What was the unmasking?" Unmasking was requested to be CENTRAL to the plot. A lot of writers included a mask, physical or metaphorical, in a perfunctory way, almost like checking a box, and that was fine, but not stellar.

Now, you may ask yourself, what did "unmasking" mean to us? That's a great question, and I wish more of the submitters had asked it. It meant that some secret had to be revealed, not to the reader, but *to at least one other character*, and the more, the better. In the stories where the revealing of a secret, and the price for it coming out, were central to the plot, we all just closed our eyes and said a silent thank you. It was astonishingly rare, and the stories that did it well received a lot more consideration.

DON'T MAKE ASSUMPTIONS. You might think, in an era of pandemic, we would have been flooded with stories about COVID-19. But, no, in the end, we were debating pulling a COVID story back from rejection, because we had so few to choose from. Our final anthology included only a single story in which the masks were COVID masks. Most people assumed we'd have tons, and so didn't write them.

EDIT YOUR WORK at Least Once. And have someone else read it at least once.

. . .

Give Me a Reason to Care. Your story should have a compelling conflict or reason for the action to take place. The more we know about this conflict in the first few paragraphs, the better.

Do Not Use a Flashback in the First Few Sentences. This is a signal you have put the beginning in the wrong place.

Do Not Open with a Character Who Has Amnesia. It is a sure-fire way to make almost any slush reader stop reading.

Do Not Include a Twist at the End That Makes a Character's Motives Finally Clear. Or, at least, don't assume doing so helps. It is nearly impossible to care retroactively for a character when we find out they're not evil or annoying after hating them the whole time. We need to care all the way through to enjoy the story. Withholding info that would help us find the main character sympathetic, just so you can feel clever, is suicide. (Note: this rule can be broken, but you better know what you're doing before trying it.) The converse is almost as true: don't reveal at the end that the main character we like the whole time is a real jerk. Unless your name is Joe Abercrombie.

. . .

Do Not Write in the Second Person. Just don't. Ditto for first person plural. Don't write in the future tense. Let your reader lose themselves in the story and forget about you, the writer, without distracting tense or person choices.

Do Another Edit for Clarity. Blocking (physical location of action and characters), timeline, cause and effect, and dialogue must all be clear *the first time through*. This is especially important if you have messed with the rules of your world (i.e. magic in your world disrupts cause and effect, or memory lapse or flashback means you're moving in different timelines).

Don't Put a Synopsis in Your Cover Letter. This might be a good idea when submitting a novel, but we are already going to read your story and don't need a synopsis. The less said about it, the better. We know the readers won't see the cover letter, so if we know too much about the stories going in, we might not trust our impressions. And it certainly sends the message that you're not confident about your prose.

Watch Made-Up Words. When you introduce a new word, you have just given your reader a job. Readers, espe-

47

cially sci-fi/fantasy readers, *like* a steep learning curve, but reading your story shouldn't feel like work. There was a great story submitted that I believe got rejected because there were four odd vocabulary words for us to memorize in the first two paragraphs.

GROW A THICK SKIN. You need to be able to separate the quality of a particular story that you wrote from your own worth. The story being awful doesn't make you awful. Once you accept this, you can *objectively* consider whether your story is, in fact, awful—which is an important thing to be able to do.

FINALLY, **don't take a rejection personally.** Being rejected doesn't necessarily mean you didn't write well enough. I learned from being on the deciding end just how true this is. There were some stories rejected for obvious reasons, but in quite a few cases, deadlines, budget, similarities in submissions, and different preferences among team members all made it obvious that we weren't picking the absolute top 21 stories. The submissions we accepted were just those that made it through our flawed process.

Read the submission guidelines. Read them again. Then follow them.

Submit a properly formatted document and your bio.

Submit early (these stories received more thorough read-throughs and consideration than those submitted just before the deadline closed).

Solidly incorporate the anthology's theme. Don't make us get out our super-secret decoder rings to puzzle over whether or not it's clear.

Edit your stories and then edit again. Have a beta reader or two give you critical feedback. Check spelling, grammar, word choice, and craft elements.

Don't waste time listing out for us what your protagonist is wearing, what his eye color is, or how tall he is. If any of these are relevant details, weave them into your prose.

Avoid the following beginnings: just waking up, answering the phone, or flashing back.

Make your first sentence hook the reader.

Do not, under any circumstances, submit your first draft.

---

1. Don't just read the guidelines. Know them. Understand them. Even commit them to memory. Make a habit out of doing this for every story that you submit. Don't assume the

guidelines are the same for every submission. Do everything that is asked of you to the T.

2. Formatting. Use proper manuscript formatting. Even the pros messed this one up. There were some stories that I just didn't want to read no matter how good the story was because of the poor formatting.

3. Revise, edit, repeat—when you're done writing, give your story to alpha and beta readers. Make sure you're turning in the best version of your story. Focus on the story in the revision. If your story is amazing, editors might overlook minor grammar problems. But editing and proofreading are a must.

4. Communication is key. If your story gets accepted elsewhere (and if simultaneous submissions are allowed), TELL THE PUBLISHERS earlier rather than later. And just communicate well with the publishers/editors in general.

5. If you get rejected, don't take it personally and attack the editors. It's a sure-fire way of getting blacklisted forever.

READ the guidelines carefully.

Choose a font easy to read.

Don't choose a bland space-filler title.

Your opening needs to be STRONG.

Make your characters memorable.

Write a proper cover letter.

Follow MS format.

Page numbers & headers are REQUIRED in the above.

Make sure your character names are consistent.

Don't rush so much you get eliminated for a stupid oversight.

Be a professional! Be kind!

Write the story our prompts inspire! Don't over think it!

Let it FLOW!

Include what genre you think your story fits in. This communicates expectations and intentions better!

---

1. This job of being an editor/slushpile reader is a highly subjective task. It's really hard to be objective. Yes, you can easily set some stories aside objectively. Poor spelling, works that haven't even been proofread, maybe totally ignoring the

guideline for using the standard manuscript style. But after that everything is much more subjective.

2. I think the *Unmasked* theme, while it seemed quite obvious to us as editors when we started this process and created the submission guidelines, was not quite as easy once we started reading. It was this nebulous thing I've seen so many times in software development. What do you want the software to do or look like? I don't know, but when I see it, I'll know it. I felt that way with these stories. Sometimes I would get caught up in a story and really love it but if I stepped back from the story, I would have to ask myself, was there really an unmasking here? Did it really fit the theme?

3. I have a feeling some of our authors didn't even consider the theme in sending in their stories. Some included a mask, but didn't really get into the Unmasking, literally or figuratively.

4. I also felt like others took a story that they had previously written, thought it fit or made some adjustments to the story and submitted it.

5. I struggled to reject a story quickly. I am pretty sure that I read completely over 80% of the stories. Many of those ended up disappointing me in the end, but I had to read to the last page because the author had hooked me in some way. Fortunately, I had plenty of reading time on my hands.

MY FINAL COMMENT. This process was both hard and easy. Having been rejected a few times myself, it was hard to write rejection letters. However, it has also made me think about my future as a publisher. As a publisher you have to think about your ability to sell a story. I tried to take that to heart when asked to pick two or three stories to consider in the final rounds. I used my best copywriting skills and my love for three stories and made my best pitch for those works. I think a publisher's belief in a story, in addition to the quality of that story, is critical to the success of a publication because I know that I can market something I believe in much, much easier than something I don't believe strongly in.

———

Follow proper manuscript format.

Read the guidelines carefully (ex. no simultaneous submissions, previously published, word count, theme, etc.)

Don't wait until the last minute to submit, since readers will be less excited by the stories. Burnout is a thing.

For slushpile readers:

Ask yourself, does this story fit the theme?

If the beginning doesn't grab you, move on.

Don't wait until the last minute to read all of the stories.

I was dismayed by how few stories I genuinely liked. But if I found myself reading without looking to see how many pages were left, then I knew I'd gotten drawn into the story. Maybe it was the sheer amount of stories that just made it difficult to really enjoy them all, so if it grabbed me in any way, then I gave it a high ranking.

Again, there were so many I forgot how many I liked! They all blur together now.

PUT in the work to become a decent writer. It was as clear as day which authors were simply vomiting words onto the page and thinking it was "writing," and which ones had studied their craft. It usually went hand-in-hand with details unrelated to writing, for example whether they knew about manuscript formatting.

It was beyond fascinating to see the truly infinite possibilities that come with writing and crafting story. This assignment—for I truly read all stories submitted—opened my eyes to more genres than I had previously been privy to.

Submit early. It is true that the early bird gets the worm. I felt not only resentful but astonished at the hundreds of stories that came in on [the] due date. It was like being hit by an avalanche—not fun.

Make your first page amazing. Precisely because of the astronomical number of submissions that came in late, I had to become more and more ruthless as time went by. I gave a story a paragraph, two, a few lines, as a chance to grab me. If they didn't do that, I rated them low and moved on.

Make your middle amazing.

Make your end amazing. I felt so disappointed at so many stories' endings. To get that far, give a story that much of my time, only to be left in disappointment-land—not good.

Is it a short story or is it a chapter of a major epic? A chapter of a major epic is not a short story. Some of the work we received would have made amazing long fiction, but did not work in the short format. Be aware of this.

For slushpile readers: try to be as ruthless as possible from the beginning. Ask yourself the simple question: does it belong in this anthology, truly? And rate accordingly.

Write the story you want to write. People writing to market or making assumptions about what everyone else will write about end up shooting themselves in the foot. Write the quirkiest, most original story you can think of, or the one in your heart, provided it fits the theme.

Don't just submit a story you've already written, change a few words to mask, and expect it to suddenly fit the Unmasked (or whichever it is) theme of the anthology. It is evident when authors did that and it infuriated me. If the story you wrote HAPPENS to fit the anthology theme perfectly—good for you! But it most likely won't. Write original.

———

ALWAYS FOLLOW PROPER MANUSCRIPT FORMAT! This was insanely frustrating to me. If someone doesn't know what that is, they can easily look it up. Proper manuscript format should be common sense, like 12-point standard font like Times New Roman, one-inch margins.

Submit your manuscript early. I was way nicer on the earlier stories than I was on the latest stories, because I had fewer submissions to read then, and I had a fresher mind.

I like a one- or two-sentence quick pitch on what the story is about so when I'm going into the final round I can remember the difference between each story without having to re-read it or write a summary for myself.

Tell us if you're a previously published author.

The biggest sad thing to me was the guy that had previously published his story and submitted anyway, which ended up making our final anthology one story short because we ultimately had to reject it. Read the guidelines. Don't submit your story if it doesn't fit the guidelines.

Don't jump back and forth between flashbacks, it gets really confusing. If I'm confused, I'm done reading.

Make sure your story fits the theme in a clear way. If I have to guess how it fits the theme, it's out.

Make your first two paragraphs the most exciting. If I finish the first two paragraphs of a short story and I'm not hooked, then I'm done reading.

SUBMIT AGAIN

Remember the old cliché, "If at first you don't succeed, then try, try again." Rejections aren't a death sentence. If your story comes back, then send it elsewhere.

And while you're waiting to hear a response from your first submission, get your next one ready to go. Write another story for a different market.

There's nothing personal about being rejected. When a form rejection letter says, "We're sorry your submission did not meet our needs at this time"—it really means, for whatever reason, that your submission did not meet their needs. It doesn't mean the editor hates you and doesn't want to hear from you ever again (well, unless you're a big-time jerk).

If you received just a form rejection or a generic response, then your story likely didn't make the first cut past the initial readers. If you do get a personal note, even just a "please try again," then your story passed at least one of the hurdles; somebody looked at it, and maybe you made the semifinals.

When my wife, Rebecca Moesta, sent her first story submission to a magazine—to an editor she knew personally —it was returned with a detailed note about some of the weaknesses along with suggestions on how she could improve the story. Rebecca was devastated and miserable, thinking the editor had a grudge against her, that her story would never make the cut, that she should throw in the towel as a writer. Having received hundreds of rejection letters myself, I was perhaps not as sympathetic as I should have been. I pointed out that it was a "good rejection" (contradictory terms in Rebecca's mind). Eventually, after a little more polishing, Rebecca did get that story published, along with other stories and books, and she's now an award-winning, *New York Times* bestselling author.

Another time, Rebecca and I were asked by a major editor to write a story specifically for a science fiction anthology he was putting together. We wrote "Collaborators," a gritty SF tale about a husband-and-wife creative team who link their minds through virtual reality to create works of art, and eventually they began to lose their own individuality. We thought it was a really good story, but the editor rejected it out of hand. "Oh, didn't I tell you? I hate virtual reality stories." We sold the story elsewhere, but we'd had no way of knowing that the story concept would lead to an immediate rejection.

I've heard of cases where a story was rejected because the main character had the same name as a hated ex-boyfriend, or the subject matter was some hot button issue—

a scene with cruelty to animals, for instance—that immediately turned the editor off.

You can't know these things. You can read the guidelines, follow the rules, put your story in proper manuscript format, adhere to the length requirements, write something in the appropriate subject or genre, and turn it in on time.

And then write another one.

And another one. Each time you'll get a little better. Remember the words of Dean Koontz: You're not wasting your time. You're learning your trade.

This is all part of the process of becoming a writer. Develop a thick skin, build up your self-confidence, and have faith in your work and your skills. After all, if you can't handle the comments from an objective editor—someone who's genuinely looking for a good story—you'll be in for a rude awakening when you do get a story or book published ... and suddenly you face the flurry of snarky Amazon reviewers or trolls who hold a grudge just because you got published and they never will.

In the meantime, do your best and good luck.

See you in the slushpile!

ABOUT THE AUTHOR

Kevin J. Anderson has published more than 170 books, 58 of which have been national or international bestsellers. He has written numerous novels in the Star Wars, X-Files, and Dune universes, as well as unique steampunk fantasy novels *Clockwork Angels* and *Clockwork Lives*, written with legendary rock drummer Neil  Peart, based on the concept album by the band Rush. His original works include the Saga of Seven Suns series, the Terra Incognita fantasy trilogy, the Saga of Shadows trilogy, and his humorous horror series featuring Dan Shamble, Zombie PI. He has edited numerous anthologies, written comics and games, and the lyrics to two rock CDs. Anderson and his wife Rebecca Moesta are the publishers of WordFire Press, and he is the Director of the Publishing MA concentration at Western Colorado University. His most recent novels are *Vengewar*, *Stake*, and *Dune: The Duke of Caladan*.

www.wordfirepress.com

IF YOU LIKED ...

IF YOU LIKED *SLUSHPILE MEMORIES*, YOU
MIGHT ALSO ENJOY:

Million Dollar Productivity
Million Dollar Professionalism for the Writer
On Being a Dictator

Million Dollar Series
Million Dollar Productivity
Million Dollar Professionalism for the Writer
Worldbuilding: From Small Towns to Entire Universes
Writing As a Team Sport
On Being a Dictator

Mr. Wells & the Martians

Resurrection, Inc.

The Saga of Seven Suns, Veiled Alliances
The Saga of Seven Suns, Whistling Past the Graveyard
The Saga of Seven Suns: TWO SHORT NOVELS:
Includes Veiled Alliances and Whistling Past the Graveyard
Three Military SF Novellas

Short Story Collections
Selected Stories: Science Fiction, Volume 1
Selected Stories: Science Fiction, Volume 2
Selected Stories: Fantasy
Selected Stories: Horror and Dark Fantasy

By Kevin J. Anderson & Doug Beason
Assemblers of Infinity
Craig Kreident #1: Virtual Destruction
Craig Kreident #2: Fallout
Craig Kreident #3: Lethal Exposure
Ignition
Ill Wind

Lifeline
The Trinity Paradox

By Kevin J. Anderson & Rebecca Moesta
Collaborators
Crystal Doors #1: Island Realm
Crystal Doors #2: Ocean Realm
Crystal Doors #3: Sky Realm

The Star Challengers Series
Star Challengers #1: Moonbase Crisis
Star Challengers #2: Space Station Crisis
Star Challengers #3: Asteroid Crisis

Kevin J. Anderson & Neil Peart
Clockwork Angels
Clockwork Lives
Drumbeats

Our list of other WordFire Press authors and titles is always growing. To find out more and to shop our selection of titles, visit us at:
wordfirepress.com

facebook.com/WordfireIncWordfirePress

twitter.com/WordFirePress

instagram.com/WordFirePress

bookbub.com/profile/4109784512

Made in the USA
Coppell, TX
15 July 2022

80022842R10046